FUSION

WHOSE POO?

POO IN THE DESERT

by
John Wood

BEARPORT PUBLISHING
Minneapolis, Minnesota

Credits:
All images are courtesy of Shutterstock.com, unless otherwise specified. With thanks to Getty Images, Thinkstock Photo, and iStockphoto.

Front Cover – VikiVector, Vektor illustration, Rosa Jay. Title typeface used throughout – PremiumVector. Vector flies – Top Vector Studio. 2 – Ksana Durand. 4–5 – Alex Vog, Tupungato, stockakia. 6–7 – Ksana Durand, mentalmind, Alexandra Lande, lady-luck, fivespots, Anan Kaewkhammul. 8–9 – baseart, Perfect_kebab, Lotta Axing, rogger design, SurfsUp. 10–11 – rchat, Jim Cumming, PACO COMO, Rosa Jay, Andrii Symonenko. 12–13 – Mircea Costina, kimman, Warren Metcalf, Sunnydream. 14–15 – COTUK_Edinburgh_BLP_HB_V2.pdf, Kuznetsov Alexey, Eric Isselee, Mr. SUTTIPON YAKHAM. 16–17 – Boston Heath, Zoltan Tarlacz, MaryValery, Panda Vector. 18–19 – Sari ONeal, fivespots, Philippe Clement, dwi putra stock. 20–21 – Raquel Pajares, fluidmediafactory, StockSmartStart. 22–23 – WildScapePhotos/Alamy Stock Photo, Mattoni et al., CC BY 2.5 <https://creativecommons.org/licenses/by/2.5>, via Wikimedia Commons, Volodymyr Voronov, Kashtanowww.

Bearport Publishing Company Product Development Team
Publisher: Jen Jenson; Director of Product Development: Spencer Brinker; Managing Editor: Allison Juda; Editor: Cole Nelson; Associate Editor: Naomi Reich; Associate Editor: Tiana Tran; Art Director: Colin O'Dea; Designer: Kim Jones; Designer: Kayla Eggert; Product Development Specialist: Owen Hamlin

Library of Congress Cataloging-in-Publication Data is available at www.loc.gov or upon request from the publisher.

ISBN: 979-8-89232-750-3 (hardcover)
ISBN: 979-8-89232-800-5 (paperback)
ISBN: 979-8-89232-837-1 (ebook)

For more information, write to Bearport Publishing, 5357 Penn Avenue South, Minneapolis, MN 55419.

CONTENTS

ALL ABOUT POO

Many deserts are full of sand and cacti, but there is also always something else. . . . It's poo! Who leaves poo in the desert? Let's find out.

Some deserts are hot and sandy, but others are cold and icy.

Don't touch any poo you find in the desert. Poo has lots of nasty things in it!

On the next pages, you will see poo in the desert. Learn about the poo, and choose which animal you think did it. Then, turn the page to find out if you were right!

ROUND AND BROWN

There's a pile of poo in the sand. Who left it here?

This poo is very hard and dry.

The droppings are round and dark brown. They look a bit like balls of chocolate.

Whose poo could it be? Choose which of these three animals you think it belongs to.

Those poos don't look that bad to me.

Camel

Oryx

Sidewinder

WHOSE POO WAS IT?

It was the camel's POO!

Camels are **herbivores,** which means they eat plants. Often, they munch on parts that other desert animals cannot eat, such as thorns and branches.

Once camels swallow food, their three stomachs **digest** it multiple times. This allows camels to take in almost all of the **nutrients** and water from the plants they eat. It is also why their poo is hard.

Camel poo comes out in clumps. The poo is so dry that it breaks apart into smaller pieces.

ROPEY POO

Who left this rope here? Wait, it's poo!

The poo is big and long. It looks like a piece of twisted, knotted rope.

This poo is full of hair and bone. Whoever made it probably eats other animals.

Whose poo could it be? Choose from these three animals.

This poo has a very **musty** smell.

The poo is out in the open. The animal probably wants it to be seen.

WHOSE POO WAS IT?

Coyotes hunt and eat other animals. Hair and bones are hard to digest, so they come out in the coyote's poo.

Coyotes use their poo to tell other coyotes to stay away. They poo out in the open to mark their **territory**.

Coyotes are awake mostly at night. This is when they hunt.

When they can't find **prey**, coyotes will eat grasses, fruits, and seeds.

POO MARKS THE SPOT

What animal left this poo in the desert grassland?

Whose poo could it be? Choose from these three animals.

This pile of pellets was left next to a hole in the ground. Where does the hole lead to?

Meerkat

Prairie dog

Desert tortoise

WHOSE POO WAS IT?

It was the prairie dog's POO!

Prairie dogs eat mostly seeds, grasses, and roots. When not out looking for food, they hide in their underground homes called **burrows**.

Many prairie dogs live together in large burrows. These connected homes are often called towns. They have lots of tunnels and rooms. There are even rooms for pooing!

The very little water prairie dogs get comes from the plants they eat. This is why their poop is dry and brown.

Prairie dogs sometimes leave poo outside burrow entrances to let other prairie dogs know someone lives there.

PEE WHERE THEY POO

Something made a real mess! Who did it?

There are bones and fur in this big poo. What does that tell you about the animal that left it?

This poo stinks!

Which of these three animals do you think made this poo?

This poo looks old and dry. The animal probably dropped it a while ago.

There is the smell of pee here, too.

Gila monster

Bobcat

I had a big lunch, but it wasn't that big!

Hamster

WHOSE POO WAS IT?

It was the **bobcat's POO!**

Bobcats are **predators**. They eat mice, rabbits, birds, and even small deer. They usually hunt early in the morning and late in the evening.

Bobcats can travel as far as 7 miles (11 km) while hunting their prey.

Bobcats may pee in the same places they poo. They use the combined smells to mark their territory and tell other animals to stay away.

BONUS POO!

NO MORE POO

Many types of scorpions live in the desert. Some can **detach** their tails if they are caught by predators. This gives them a chance to escape.

A detached scorpion tail can still wriggle and sting.

However, scorpions poo out of the end of their tails. This means that once their tails break off, the critters can never poo again.

Scorpions can detach their tails in three places.

After about eight months without tails, these scorpions die from a buildup of poo in their bodies.

GLOSSARY

burrows underground tunnels or holes made by animals to live in

detach to separate a part from its whole

digest to break down food into things that can be used by the body

herbivores animals that eat only plants

musty smelling of wetness or decay

nutrients natural substances that plants and animals need to grow and stay healthy

pellets small, hard balls of poop or undigested food

predators animals that hunt and eat other animals

prey animals that are hunted and eaten by other animals

territory the area where an animal lives and finds its food

INDEX